Contents

CW01507903

Beyond the Rivers

Faruk Šehić
My Rivers

My Rivers

Poems by
Faruk Šehić

Translated
from the Bosnian by
S.D. Curtis

Originally published as
Moje Rijeke, Buybook, 2014

Copyright © Faruk Šehić, 2023
Translation copyright
© S.D. Curtis, 2023

The right of Faruk Šehić, to
be identified as the author of
this work has been asserted in
accordance with the Copyright,
Designs and Patents Act, 1988

First published in 2023
by Istros Books
London, United Kingdom
www.istrosbooks.com

Typesetting: pikavejica.com

Cover art:
Aleksandra Nina Knežević

Printed by CMP,
Poole, Dorset, UK

ISBN: 978-1-912545-35-3

The publishers wish
to express their thanks to
Arts Council England

Supported using public funding by
ARTS COUNCIL
ENGLAND

This is the Serchio
whose waters have been drawn
for perhaps two thousand years
by my peasant folks
by my father and my mother

Giuseppe Ungaretti, from 'Rivers', 1916
Translated by Diego Bastianutti

Forget your personal tragedy. We are all bitched from the start and you especially have to be hurt like hell before you can write seriously. But when you get the damned hurt use it — don't cheat with it ... All we are is writers and what we should do is write.

(from Hemingway's letter
to F. Scott Fitzgerald, 1934)

The Loire

Liberation Day

I walked the sandy shore a few miles
A rough line of shells marked the tide's border
mostly resembling the heads of aliens
The Atlantic floods the French coast
which sounds like a tautology but isn't
Flooding can be a happy repetition
of breaking waves and mild climate
I recognized the washed-out indigo of mussels
lodged in the sand like helmets of cosmic Lilliputians
People and their dogs ran alongside the ocean
Imagination blown every which way

Here the Americans and British
disembarked in two world wars
Here in the bay the HMS Lancaster sunk
in 1940, with the loss of 4000 souls
Fraternal flags flutter proudly on masts
(two of the few that I can stomach)
Respect is the only thing I can feel
imagining American warships
in the centre of Saint Nazaire
The menacing grey of steel determined
to defend the world from Nazism
Here was the USS Saratoga, whose name
I loved as a child, the river waters
softening the smell of the ocean

A chill wind blows off the distant sea
under my feet the husks of dead shells rustle
Today is Liberation Day
Wreaths are laid at the monuments
to fallen soldiers and brave French civilians
On the open sea, cargo ships glide
murky waves of Biblical significance
here the river and ocean become one
Wet encrusted sand along the shore
Imagination blown every which way

I would like someone to call my name
for the wind to call me *Faroukh*
as the Arabs and the French say it
so that finally I belong somewhere
and bond with a new place
I'd grow a sailor's beard and catch
small silver fish in my net
from a boat that coughs steam and oil
I feel far from Sarajevo
my heavy, tortuous love
an addiction, an obsession, as physical
as precious scars from long-ago battles

Now I am the broad Loire flowing
from the Atlantic beneath my terrace
I join with the salt water
thirsty for the ocean's expanse
Only the sound of shells crunching beneath my feet
returns me to the windswept Atlantic
I'm free to live forever or to die at this moment
without remorse, with double

human experience heavy within me
This thought passes briefly through my head
stopping me short
before I continue along the sandy shore
as if nothing had happened
all wars briefly forgotten

And so I surrender to the huge wave
that rises from the heart of the planet
passing through fish eyes and human blood cells
rustling in the evenings through soft plant leaves
transforming me into a nightingale
a simple bird that sings of the melancholy
of an endless shore – of children's sandcastles
left to the mercy of Atlantic wind
of clips holding tight the hair of freckled girls
of victories and everyday defeats
of the boundless joy in my chest
for which I would rush unarmed
to defend the flimsiest ideal
a joy that invokes in me the sweet childish scent of your skin
to bring me doubly alive, at one with all the sailors
who emerge from the deep

I, a sailor who has never left dry land
will be at my best leading the drowned
the dismembered and those burnt
in the blazing oil of warships
sailors dragged by sharks
into the boiling bubbling blue dizzying air
and those crippled ones with long seaweed beards
that the sea has claimed as its own

Scales now grow on their skin
and their hands become seal fins
I could lead such sea centaurs ashore
in a final breakthrough towards the light
Strange what power suffering can bring a man
(the downtrodden know this too well)
Proletariat of the seas, drunkards and troublemakers
young American marines en-route to Normandy
vomiting with fear as they disembark from landing craft
in uniforms that will become funeral shrouds
Such men I would like to lead
into the ultimate battle, into the resurrection
of green grass beneath clear skies
without the salvos of heavy naval guns
without the screech of aeroplanes
or the confusion of anti-aircraft fire
without those shadowy submarines
like long Antarctic whales
seen from high-flying planes
Fragile dandelion parachutes
would be all that would fall

Strange how suffering can distort a man
grant him the atomic strength of the survival instinct
All those small earthly battles we endured
wounded, crippled and raped
All those tiny defeats that made me stronger
that daily dose of hemlock, of which I drank more
than Christ on the cross
Strange how pain becomes an integral part of the body
On the French Atlantic coast, on a wing of wind
which carries me along the sandy shore

I saw my future love
a woman strong yet gentle
a mermaid with a seaweed crown
Until then I will lead bloated sailors
amalgams of human and starfish
I'll win forgotten lost battles and rewrite history
in favour of the humiliated and the slain
Until I watch the surface of the sea from below
weary and sleepy, falling through the deeps
like plankton illuminated by sunbeams
abandoning all with open arms
and palms forever pierced by harpoons
wrought with love
Until the sea makes us whole again.

Ripening

There are days for crying
for rearranging your biography
One drawer is humid, with grass growing inside
each blade the same length
its roots poking through the veneer, boring
on into the pure tissue of ash
Caress that grass as if were the hair of your firstborn
all is well in that drawer
for grass produces silence and oxygen
No human faces lie there, persistent in their gaze
curious, discouraging, distorted faces
with broken teeth, crooked noses, blood-shot eyes
Close the drawer, let the grass create its world in you
A sphere of green

There'll be more dark days
for rearranging your biography
When the rain pours down from distant stars
a monster in each drop
a stranger, a stellar lifeform, falling, falling
like a rose unaware of its own scent
Black rain falls, coal and sludge from distant stars
where spikey miners tirelessly load celestial trolleys
their wheels heavy and powerful
while diesel engines sing
Fires burn even in the hearts of the frozen
but remembering love gone by
brings brief warmth, a single firelighter

Never stray too far from your grave
listen to it breathe, this mound
which hasn't yet ripened
into a brotherhood of soil and grass
Oh, how I love the soil!
Those inexplicable particles, worthless dust
magic dust from which everything sprouts
your beard, your jawbone
the origin of everything
I saw your upper lip in the black soil before I saw it on your face
I wanted to pluck its soft purple, rip it from its earthly roots
but I'd no strength for that
I stopped breathing for a moment
my hands went numb, my blood stopped coursing
I'd reached for the untouchable harmony of earthly hues

There are days for crying
for chanting strangers' names
down beneath the roots
in that darkness greater than the swelling sky
across the seven celestial seas
names that will be borne by future faces
you don't see them yet
but they're down among the tubers
smelling of manure and lilies
fresh beef lard, a carved wooden bowl
faces of people you will yet meet
and love like none before
always like the first time, loving them anew
You've discovered that secret
the elixir on the tip of your tongue
the electric shock of a kiss
Now you're finally ready for your dark days.

A Tune Lost in The Night

My body was naked and feeble
the body of a jellyfish washed ashore
Soft jelly-cake rolled in sand
that's what the first one I found looked like
I wanted to return her to the ocean
to revive her with the tip of my shoe
trying to push her back, unaware
the waves had thrown her out dead
Later I came across four more
all the same species, with a brown core
and one long whiplike tendril
They became two-dimensional, sinking into the sand
My warring monster would say they looked like anti-tank mines
circular with antennae, blades of wild grass
turning armoured vehicles into scrap metal
It was the open sea and the white gulls that distracted me
from my monster's gaze

The botanical garden was deserted
all things were serving melancholy
Painted old women with loud flowers in their hair
cypresses, yellow-billed thrushes
baroque benches of braided iron
cast as playful ivy
In a botanical garden sadness is banned
plants blossom with all the perfumes of the world

A ship passes across the bay, a skyscraper
laid flat along the green swinging waves, a building-boat
steered by a passenger's dreams
For a moment I thought I could walk on water
that river mermaids held me afloat
with their palms polished white by the tides
The lights go on in the shipyard
lighthouse beams flicker on the breakwaters
time to return home, where the body is protected
time to rid myself of scales
sprouting thought-forms
to sit on the terrace, open a beer
toast the eternity we are part of
that small, daily eternity of restorative seconds
to become a happy cog in the mechanism of night

A ship's siren fills my soul
deep as the Pacific, mournful as a whale's sigh
I long to write a poem that agitates
the maelstrom of loneliness
A poem to fill someone's soul
with the silicone of dead jellyfish, sprinkled
with rose petals from the botanical garden
and endless bursts of sighing.

Ocean-river or Vice Versa

I can think what I will of the Loire
that it is larger than the sky
that it shows the sky itself, a refuge for archetypal creatures
that it flows into the ocean as the Atlantic flows into it
bringing salt water deep into the continent.
Whipped by wind, it is the Sea of Atlas
condemned by Zeus to forever carry the earth
after siding with the Titans against Olympian gods
Atlas wasn't thrown to Tartarus, that unimaginable abyss
he was forced to hold us on his shoulders
(we who know human nature, know there's no greater punishment)
Before my eyes, the waters turn green when calm
but murky if the Bora wind rises
and fishermen drive their long rods into the sandy shore
to catch eels, while hooded walkers
eyes downcast, fight against the gale
This poetic river, this poetic ocean
greater than anything I've ever seen
is a watery tomb for people and ships
At the bay of Saint-Nazaire, civilians and soldiers lie
an entire Srebrenica underwater
Lord have mercy on their souls
Today the wind lifts
sand erasing innocent footprints
The shadows of kites rushing headlong through the dunes
the tides scatter thousands of shells along the shore

a temporary mausoleum of fragile armour
I can think whatever I will about the Atlantic
that it is greater than humanity, the sum of its dreams
when I'm far away I'll respect it even more
that sea of a punished god
able to wash away worldly grief
drown out the sound of our fighting
revive our hopes with a single wave
The tear of a god banished
forever there, on the shores of the Atlas Sea
I will cover myself with sand as if it's newspaper
put black shells on my eyelids
without the superfluous magic of words
merging ocean and river.

Another Loire

Solitude shrink-wraps me
Weaning myself off other people, I struggle
with addiction to another's body
remove her face from my memory
shoot it beyond earth's orbit
Ashes to ashes, cosmic dust to cosmic dust
Souls need forgetting
protection from memory's airy chambers
Like worn-out shirts, souls become threadbare
We can discard them all and still death continues
to bribe us with new faces, with old money
bargaining with your feelings
yet it habituates you to solitude's existence
The fewer people you know
the fewer faces you owe to death
Last night I made love with Valérie
her body was a nuclear reactor, smooth
tattooed, I know that addiction to someone special
the difficulty of forgetting
someone encountered in the night
Imagine the pain when remembered
faces are all that is left of us
Once the body has been
buried, does hair still grow for its own sake?
Night falls in Paris
beneath the earth nothing happens
In a little while even hair will stop growing

death renders its efforts pointless
a face can pale with time, but cannot be erased
Memory is full, those shirts long worn-out
while bodies continue to decompose
The fewer people you know
the fewer faces you owe to death
Valérie is warm, she is real
Night falls in Paris
beneath the earth nothing moves.

The Spree

Émigré Soul

If I could afford to, I'd post myself to Berlin
with DHL or FedEx. I weigh around 85 kilos
and Berlin would cost, I'll borrow the lot
there are always people with cash
and it's important I reach Berlin in a DHL parcel
I've decided against FedEx, the company's name is too long
it rhymes with those Bosnian firms whose owners think
success is the internationalism of an *ex*
I'll post myself to the Hauptbahnhof, I've been before
I can find my way, being familiar with the U-
Bahn, its enticing smell
I'm hooked on the odour of the Berlin underground
promising speed and good times
I must post myself to Berlin
touch the Brandenburg Gate
caress the stone buttocks of Greek goddesses
the colour of milky coffee sipped in Potsdamer Platz
serenaded by sparrows, those feathery balls
navigating the glass domes of arcades
strung with sails or what seem now like sails, now
like neckties made for giants
Those sparrows surround me as I drink
in the late sun, they'll wait for crumbs
while I sit in the garden of an exotic restaurant
(serving crocodile steak and koala fillet)
Berlin is a city where history can't give you a headache

undigested, this thought cleanses me as I walk over the dead
German and Allied soldiers, or rather their skeletons
fragmented on the lawn in front of the Reichstag, by the river Spree
where real eagles execute a fly-pass
while beneath the grass history
lies transparent, I am hell-bent on escaping Sarajevo
I must post myself to Berlin in a cardboard box marked *Urgent!*
I'll rid myself of shop-soiled nations and stunted statelets
my blond hair, these green eyes will help me get through
X-ray control, although I wasn't born in Berlin
they'll know I've got a mysterious watermark on my irises
a biometric passport of a state, a borderless state
not yet created, but still
until it comes into being
Berlin will do me just fine.

The Spree

Dark and turbid river
flowing slowly like melting anthracite, here and there
the current shows its muscles, the water
rolls in oily swirls
turning in on themselves
all that the surface collects
images of skies and riverbanks
The Spree is dangerous
you cannot see your own face in it
The riverbed is as far from you as the famine in Somalia
framed on the news
Oh, those Ray-Ban frames
through which I survey the suffering world!
The riverbed is out of reach, even for a bionic arm
the kind worn by a boy born limbless
a boy who wrote to Mercedes
for a new kind of arm
(that they provided, along with their logo)
The Spree is dark, just as I imagine
the depths of German forests
while I travel with the ICE train
images of Teutonic mythology running
through my mind
Schwarzwald is the guilty word
conjuring dark German forests, the particular
paradox of pretty pink teenage bodies, mostly blond
dancing with carefree smiles on a hired boat

while the Spree remains
an object of desire, untouchable
its water so polluted they've banned bathing
The desire of the young bodies fascinates
with the impossibility of diving
into the water, to become
one with the black, murky Spree.

Blood Tribute

There was too much expectation
too much hope and the belief in a new life
What we wished for has turned against us
try as I might, along with the caterpillars in Görlitzer park
and the punks at Kottbusser Tor, everything went
against the feelings I had for you
Too much longing and passion to fit two bodies
The moustaches of melancholy Turks
the rotating kebabs, conical planets
orbiting their axes, everything I saw
sad scenes, dirty streets
people wrapped up warm
there were no words to explain
what went wrong
Lovers of tragedy that we are
the creators of empty dramas
At Treptower Park we argued in English
under the Red Army monument
On the stone plaque commemorating Soviet victory
Stalin lectured Hitler in German, but I didn't care
I cared only about retracting
into her body, launching us
into a run with hands clasped
English was not our language of love
From my kitchen window I watched the night circle Kreuzberg
A perfect light blue backdrop for departure
Berlin remains cold and distant

tight in my delusion that a stranger can understand me
without touching my pain
I must go south, among the swallows that chirp
above the Miljacka river, their throats
trumpets sounding out deep blue evenings
Because we didn't know the end was really the start
something bigger than either of us
than either Sarajevo or Berlin
And this heartbeat that I love
I would allow to kill me.

Waiting for the Saviour 11.07.2011

For the first time in my life, I couldn't feel the city
Destroyed and confused in Kreuzberg
I drank for hours
moving from bar to bar among young naïve tourists
their large rucksacks heavier than their small brains
That didn't stop me joining them for a drink
I looked right through them, they hovered
transparent as Antarctic jellyfish
I couldn't even pity them, as I pitied myself
lost in a city I'd fetishized, I understood
alienation means you are not seen by others
yet you see a saviour in each of them
The Messiah won't approach with soothing words
you are a hologram to him in a world of black
metal smelted from working-class Balkan sweat
I fell asleep in a clean hostel
paying more for the privilege of sleeping alone
the morning brought cold rain, compassionless skies
An army rucksack on my back, my laptop in hand
I began to hate Berlin, to curse it
(I'm lying: I whispered sweet nothings)
On Platform Two I waited for the train to Munich
Sixteen years ago, the genocide in Srebrenica began
my heart was breaking, there was no one to save me
twenty-eight hours Berlin-Munich-Zagreb-Sarajevo
My silence is an antenna reaching out to the Big Bang

33

A void for my head like the iced snowballs of childhood
Two thousand kilometres in one haul
When I arrived at my local bar
my usual chair on the terrace was empty and I knew
I was home, where even darkness can be comfortable.

The Drina

Our Bodies are Beautiful Infernal Machines

25th May, 2006, this morning
bitterness tied around my neck, a millstone
that can't be washed away with coffee and cigarettes
nor by the dew-sweet air
We've become functional human bodies
our ancestors boiling
through the ruins we hold inside, all those
iron-heavy burdens
like pale worms I pulled from the skulls of calves
beneath the old slaughterhouse on the banks of the Una
bait for catching grayling and trout
back before war broke out
Too many bloody histories lurk in each of us
I enjoyed Vienna just last year
finding myself in the metro early morning, a carriage that sped
faster than a meteor
watching the harmonious swaying plastic handles
strung along the metal rails
like the nooses in ropes for hanging twenty in a row
swinging to and fro
This morning bitterness
turns into prehistoric rage, into the dark
Apocalypse of St John, into the black earth
like the coffee dregs
from which cyclamen and wild strawberries grow
in a water cross made by the over-flowing

stream at a bog near the town of Srebrenik
Yet these are only literary reminiscences
with which I stubbornly defend myself
with which we all stubbornly defend ourselves
from a non-metaphorical Bosnia
which gently murders us.

A Return to the Garden of Eden

What remains of poetry
after you cease to believe in it
Gone are the emotions you wielded
both great and irrelevant
now the stumps of day and night
The inability to master a metaphor without ego
because it abolishes itself for the sake of another's glory
The hypocrisy of writing once
avoided by sparing words from which poetry can be made
when the time is right
Blood you turned into the sweet wine of night
brutality as innate in you as a speech impediment
sustaining you in a brittle world, faith
in words like brotherhood, human, solitude
A planet can be immense, or
fit into your pocket
If the pursuit of love is not the secret meaning of life
a fundamental colour is missing from the spectrum
text messages of the dead
the signs which you alone see
the arabesques of birds in flight
the tumour on the face of a clerk
growing like tree fungus
grubby gypsy kids beside the Eternal Flame
a three-dimensional tapestry of Sarajevo
Fascism that never changes, never

growing old, conformity
the succulence of a vagina, at your touch
like a butcher who loves the smell of fresh meat under his nails
Revolutionary ideas you discarded like old shoes
Your body has become accustomed to the scars
inflicted by hatred, by envy
Writing athletic prose, you can convert money to satisfaction
Will I be content now that I don't write poetry, now
the form and repetition of words no longer bothers me
Language fatigue, nerve fatigue
all that disgusts me in my work and that of others
What is poetry, did it emerge before the Big Bang
I don't look for the answer in the flickering
shadow of an oil lamp, nor the melancholy moon
I give myself to the days and nights that come
from time and space, all the places I've lived
Childish flights of fancy
when life can bewitch a man with the weight of repeated actions
an automatism of the soul
and the jungle of trivia
Then again, one might call it happiness
to be free, healthy and strong
liberated from suffering, longing, from unfulfilled wishes
Now that nothing happens, perhaps there is poetry
nothing magnificent, not pregnant as history
splattered with the blood of the illiterate
the photo of a warm corpse
haunting the consciousness of an idle Westerner
I lost my excess bile along the way
I'll leave poetry to those who'll pay the price
True poetry, without human sacrifice
endless warfare and memoranda overloading

mass graves, I can see it
in your muscular body
in the green of your iris and your embrace
not only does the world cease to exist
we return to where we were exiled from.

Animal Epistle

I can go hungry for days
although I see no point in asceticism
Once I starved myself out of curiosity
awaiting a miracle, a revelation in front of my eyes
the final fruit from the Tree of Knowledge
Yet nothing shows itself as a shining example
and nothing is better than a false discovery
Hunger made my senses sharper
I tested them, gauged their limits
One moment, I became simply my own senses
lucid, strong and fast, able to kill prey with my teeth
I wasn't aware of the great philosophers, only Emerson
who said that Gothic cathedrals imitated the great forests
Hunger would turn me sharp as a blade
I'd walk into town and mingle with people
who wouldn't suspect a thing from my outward stance
while inside, I'd feel each tiny vibration of asphalt
each passing tram shaking the soil in flowerpots
each vowel on the lips of passers-by
wild as war crime committed by ordinary people
conspiratorial rustlings from consonants on the teeth
the engorging of jugular veins
I'd feel my teeth growing, the saliva inside my mouth
bursting with digestive enzymes
I could even write poems, then
replete with bloody chunks of meat

beneath the saddles of Tatar horsemen
I could do so many things, yet hesitated
before the orgasmic star-jump
When I started eating, there was no stopping me
I'd devour cities, neon towers, shopping centres
where the mind outlives its miserable fate
Like a candle burning in a poorhouse
I would make offerings to myself
unbaked lamb legs washed down with wine, rakia
and cigarettes in which time burned out
I can go hungry for days
quiet as the Northern Lights
I'll become pure, I am
Catharsis, have we met?
I drink hemlock in your stead
I kill for you, love for you my heart beating
faster, I crucify myself daily
and will be resurrected when no-one has need of me.

The Waste Industry

Things are produced to become rubbish
In the absence of a future, imaginary
shells continue to fall on Sarajevo
I bought myself a cheap imaginary bullet-proof vest
just in case, at the flea market of broken dreams
where ordinary life begins
They say those killed at Markale Market were just puppets
Strange no politician is killed randomly
proclaimed a rag doll, I could have been
called by a different name, that would've changed
nothing, neither the character of the war nor the collective
trauma, here your name is not a sign
it's the password for genocide
the Drina no longer a river, but a flowing memorial
Things are produced only to become rubbish
Humans, for instance, don't last long
I knew as much even as I was hiding
beneath my own hair
Combs from Buchenwald have lost their hair forever
the Nazis were systematic down to the last
detail: classifying lice into small, medium and large
With industrial zeal they turned humans, human
hair into heavy clouds, they killed God in Man forever
Adam and Eve resided in the Omarska camp
after their stay in Auschwitz
I love things because they delineate the shifting

space of sorrow, I fall
in love with things, pampering them
and weeping when they are damaged or destroyed
Skips are full of discarded things
cloth strewn as in a mass grave
Once upon a time things had their stardom
their Hollywood glamour, charity
balls for the hungry children of the black continent
Now they burden the earth
with their crippled existence, just
like the human race.

A Walk through Srebrenica

When I first went to Srebrenica
piercing air thick as gelatine
I walked through a town that had moved
underground, with more stray dogs than people
on the streets, everything I saw
transformed into something else
A house here is not like other houses, here
the landlord is Death
The flora was foreign, although
I recognised each plant and all that I saw
seemed like a reminder of things from long ago, so
deeply did the news images imprint on my memory
The force of gravity slows steps and language
each visit is a pilgrimage, especially the first
grass-grown and tongue-tied
I had to let blood on the way back to Sarajevo
let the night pulse
play with my body and release
the pain, only then could I tell the discrepancy
between physical strength and the bitterness
that is defeat
Once I went to Srebrenica
from the opposite direction, from Belgrade
I began with an allergic attack
a fear of death by suffocation
then I walked through the streets of Srebrenica

cured, I had returned home
to the blackest heart of darkness
The windows were dark mirrors, loneliness
drifted from each chimney instead of a rope of smoke
Here the dreaded silence is the fifth element
the voice of those who are no more
I imagined the houses were living
beings to inhabit this place with life
inside my head
The stream murmured between empty dwellings
behind curtains darkness released its mycelia
while the souls of the dead silvered
bare brick houses swung past me
deep into the night
A huddled cat on the stone steps
furry spring of warmth
and a single quince
left to ripen on the stairway
A night walk through Srebrenica fills me with hope
The stars of salvation restore my dignity of being
When I was in Srebrenica
I felt a colossal confusion
a Godless universe
The weight of my body carried here was a punishment
Yes, guilt is the air we exhale
No poem about Srebrenica will ever end, infinite
sadness is its subterranean hum
The heritage of our souls

Erfurt Memories

The feeling haunts me, how to describe
with words that sound stereotyped
Nazism and the shadow it throws across nowadays Germany
In Erfurt we visited the memorial where the crematoria were built
JA Topf & Söhne supplied the death industry
Crematoria in the nearby KL Buchenwald had company marks
and with reason, for in the Middle Ages, Erfurt
synagogue was burnt down, the Jews were killed
systematically: nothing comes out of the blue
there is always a societal medical history
a spiral of collective breakdowns
Sleepiness overcame me in the place
where stoves were built to smelt people
A bewildered curator attempted to explain while we made
        light of it
disgust bored through me, disgust and a black curtain
that's Germany in a few words
Horror soon leaves one hungry, the stomach pushes out
death, my hunger made me sick
but my sandwich and the bland dessert made me sick too
It's hard to wash the taste of turkey and bloody redcurrants
out of one's mouth, the flame of hatred
smoulders for centuries, the smoke from the crematorium
winds through my windpipe precisely
because of my innocence
my sympathy, simple humanity

Disgust and a black curtain, better yet
a heavy sheet, let it be brocade
the size of present-day Germany with gaps
for sunshine, where Germans remained innocent
with the thickest black material to cover the Nazi dens
Gothic cathedrals in Gothic towns
blacken with earth, incinerate
history where glorious kings rest in vaults
Never before has grandiose history
crashed to earth as here
Nation, purity, fatherland: the incantations of the Holocaust
Can't you see the geometric valleys and gingerbread villages
the demonic peasants with their ruddy cheeks?
Let the black cloth cover it all
except the Alps and the dazzling whiteness
on your way to Scandinavia.

A Glass Marble from Potočari

When the dead cannot speak of themselves
not even a whimper
order the soil to be moved into the landslide of ideas
into the twilight of the twentieth century
Or raise tidal waves of metal and glass
let grey snow fall
like the ashes from Buchenwald
But yet again, nothing happens
The grass is worldly indifference
combed over their eyes
like holy green hair
A victim is a victim
with no language, forever
dead, the same body killed several times
with heavy machines, heavy
oblivion in primary, secondary, tertiary
mass graves and a dayless abyss

Before being shot
the body, as if diving into a lake
will hold its breath but
lets fly to sunlit hills, those treetops
where future events shadow themselves already
Our song falls apart
the dead have lost the words
to start their story over

Let the silvery voices say:
Evil conquered us this time

Once I remembered Buchenwald
in a Buddhist monastery
the hustle and bustle, the sweat and thyme
I burst out crying, and could not stop
They say the soul of the world is strong, when
in the leaves of Buddha's tree
I almost saw his face, convinced
tears can defend us from what is
senseless, just as a woman in Potočari told me
once in a field of white headstones:
Children are not mushrooms

I found my salvation in a glass marble
that had survived the shooting in a pocket
the only sign of life left in a horizontal body
the hard calm of the glass
its colours the flags of indestructible cities
of sun and fire
its blue stripe the smile of the ocean
The man who had warmed it in his pocket
free of this sorrowful world
Only in a poem can you bring back the dead.

Bosnia Ltd. 1992

My homeland is a geographical triangle
inhabited by cynical castoffs
founded on three nationalities
with Jews, Roma and Others
Damned nations hate themselves first, then the others
yet the question remains
who is the other
They wake each morning with eyes full of crusty hatred
those bastards who take hatred to bed and grave
In the animal kingdom there's no catharsis
but knife, bullet, fire and suffering
but they eat and drink to excess
and love God too fervently
When nations are at war and gods wear camouflage fatigues
they all have their own deity
My homeland is
the gleam of a bayonet at dawn on Monte Melleti
the Corpus Christi of repeated crucifixions
From East and West they've continually sought blood
now they butcher in three parts
to satisfy bellies born of ancestral hunger
Their souls swim in the grease of lamb, beer, rakia and pork
their imaginations rotting in the apple from the pig's mouth
eating and drinking, slaughtering to be closer to God
My homeland is
a beautiful tomb for people and ideas, chlorophyll blue

Our Faces, Mass Grave, Remix

Bones are not attractive
even when you write about them.
Even through paper, the odour seeps
Making the reader squirm in remembering
that hunchbacked cousin of war
that everyone's ashamed of

Bones are not attractive
not an angelic voice on the X Factor
not some new pornographic music clip
not a politician's living room
or his toothy wife and children in a glossy magazine.
They are distant from all of this
from bones that still stink after twenty years
damned bones, that never rot
and this earth that keeps spitting them out
so that dogs still find skulls
in the centre of town

Bones are not attractive
They have nothing
of the glamour of the jet-set
don't stimulate the collective imagination
and are no longer profitable.
Once one could profit from them
millions of German marks in the private pockets

of those close to the Father of the Nation
whose children attend prestigious international colleges
Mischievous little devils in Prada

Bones are not attractive
mummified in mass graves
even when you build an Entity* on them
Every layer they strip
Seems camped on before
Seamus Heaney didn't know what he wrote
in his 'Door into the Dark'
I know and you know. They don't know
(*This country belongs to us*, to all our dead)
Bosnia is covered with bones.

*   'Republika Srpska' is one of the two entities of Bosnia and Herzegovina, the other being the Federation of Bosnia and Herzegovina. Officially 'Republika Srpska' was recognized in the 1995 Dayton peace agreement, but it was formed in 1992 as a result of ethnic cleansing, war crimes and genocide.

Domestic Epiphany

I'd like to write about Srđan Aleksić
something great, bombastic, that delicate
souls would weep over
but then I recall other comrades
beneath the earth, unrecognized, forgotten
and I know their restlessness woke me
in deaf times
dipped me in the world's blood, used me as a quill
Those who loved life beside the river Una
died so we could return to our town, our desire
our greatest weapon, only families of the dead remember that
Liberation Day is the anniversary of his death
twenty cosmic minutes afterwards
I'd like to write about Srđan Aleksić
but I don't know how
I've not recorded my comrades' heroic deaths
in an useless war, they were misspent coins
paying for superhuman victories
cancelled by the need for coexistence
for forgiveness, a bright future that forgets
the words were false, devoid of comfort
twenty cosmic minutes afterwards

It is the end of January
a dry winter wind blows snow like icing
sugar on the anniversary of Srđan Aleksić's death
There's revolution in Ukraine, depression in Sarajevo
nothing else to write home about
I'm sorry I've no more flowers at home
I'd water them now, although I watered them this morning
I'd dedicate myself to them
Srđan would prune yellow leaves with nickel-plated scissors
encourage the buds to develop into flowers
invite the sun to show us the miracle of photosynthesis
Removed from the outside world
he coexisted with plants, spoke
the mysterious language of greenery
How stupid it is to try redeeming
survivors, feeling guilty because we survived
My gardenia jasmine shrugged its shiny leaves
the winter sun has no zenith
a brief shadow creeps across the sky

Indoor plants need more water, their soil
inspected for mould and aerated with a silver fork
their worn-out pots regularly changed.

My House is of Star Tufa

It's twenty-two years since I first
became a refugee, I say first
because you never know when
you might be left once
again, with only the shirt on your back
If only people were like snails
carrying their homes on their backs
instead of bundles and rucksacks
that will fray, as everything frays
with age, to die not once but many times
which implies a chain of eternal resurrection
I'll mourn everyday things the most
the photo album without which I am a ghost
expelled from the homeland of sorrow
The question is did I ever stop being a refugee?
If I carried onto the battlefield
just an old army backpack with a pair of socks
it was pointless to carry things, crawling
towards death, minimalism was my motto
I would enter death prepared
ascetically, so no-one had to bother
about my corpse, and that's how
I entered the peace

As a tenant I had a survival kit
I didn't invest in comfort: bed, table, chair
laptop, fridge, bath, boiler and clothes
What more do you want?
If they start shooting
I'm ready to put everything on my back
to be a refugee again, whoever
must become a refugee once
wanders until death, maybe beyond
the cosmos is the only true home
I know no other homeland.

Beyond
the Rivers

Revolution is an Odyssey

I shouldn't have thrown away the old things
pressed petals from creased notebooks
those books signed by anonymous authors
I shouldn't have
disturbed dust's harmony, the particles of my skin
or the skin of those I loved
in this comfortable lair, I shouldn't have
embarked on such a revolution
with such unforeseen consequences, once you
break the secret order of things, once
you touch the placenta of the hidden cosmos
and tear the spider's webs
entwining the past, it all goes to hell
Your actions are irreversible, unlocking
the mechanism of melancholy, invisible
guns are turned on you, agents and killers track you
down, your heart pounds
you can't escape, wherever you look
your memories have been infiltrated
you see the face you loved
in the concave mirror of a spoon
Drawing water into a cistern
a whole life of action
seeps away, in vain
you seek to hide in your habits
in banal rituals executed on low pedestals

The desire to overcome your melancholy
does not make you guilty
You removed the dust and the old things, then
the real revolution began and you
embarked on it thoughtlessly
despite knowing the war had worn you
out, yet revolution is ultra-erotic
and the streets are full of young people
ready for anything, simply anything
Revolution's motto is blood, tears, sweat and sperm
And as always, you emerge
poorer than before, the revolution
consumes too much, you
lost the wife that left when the gardenia flower
dried out on the windowsill of the glass terrace
you gave all for the revolution, it gave nothing
in return, the shrivelled leaves of that gnarled plant
and the belly of a dead boiler on the wall
It took away your wife, threw her
into the arms of a certain counter revolutionary
Revolutions are like pigs eating everything in their path
yet men are the biggest swine
When you are wounded, when your guts
leak over the whitest snow
replace them with pig's intestines, together
in digestive fraternity
that nameless pig and you, so
don't make small revolutions in your own den
for your home town will soon revolt
when it does, barricade yourself in your flat
pretend you don't see parliament burning
stockpile food, water and candles

wait for it to pass, hidden
but kiss your wife as if every time were the last
Don't allow them to fraternize you with pig intestines
for neither you nor the pig will benefit
It all began with innocence, a lack of pomp
You have disturbed the mysterious order of things
now you must face the consequences
There is no other way
but the cross on your back
and the road up ahead.

A War of Final Reconciliation

Centuries away from your kiss
from the smoke that binds houses to the sky
and the plants on the windowsills, war is
a return to the Stone Age by other means
those were the days corpses were valuable
I can't remember when
that battlefield was categorized grammatically
My dirty fingers touched your scarf as I inhaled
retaining what was still innocent
Wounded, asleep, we
dragged ourselves through primeval mud
step by step, a column, a giant's thread, a worm
stitching through the festering wound, this
never-ending war, this murmur of weeping
willows on riverbanks in bitter twilight
Dandelions blaze in our palms like flares now
we retreat half alive and half
dead, there will be no return
ash-grey villages and towns, burnt metropolises on stars
no one is spared among the bacteria
the holy spirit, divine sperm
Everyone dies a thousand times, only we expect
a pardon, holy shadow, gallows of the world
your blonde hair burns like the horizon at dawn
It will burn like this house
in enemy territory a girl said:

If only your hair would burn like this house
That was back when I didn't know you existed
when the rivers began to cut through limestone and sandstone
I dream of a line of trees at the end of the world
I walk in a raincoat of brilliant leaves
full of wonder for living things: ants, snails, robins
for those lovesick warriors from the songs of Leonard Cohen
Multi-coloured eucalyptus cannons
will launch us into space.

Manifesto

Golden grass in the sun, never-ending
childhood, that small vessel of warm cruelty
here we learnt what life was
about dissected frogs in biology class, performed
gymnastics on the pommel horse
Stars above the soft earth, the blinding sun
Rivers flowed as best they could
leaves rustled each evening as heat
abated: fish, birds, earthworms, ants, crickets
I'll never forget those creatures
nor the rainbow trout I caught on the spinnerbait
struggling so hard it flew across my head into the quince tree
The sculpins prodded with straightened forks
looked like Poseidon's trident
Under a lifted stone, you had to be quick
to catch a sculpin
plunging the fork into its body
careful not to kill it, threading it
onto the hook, to lure the trout

The world has always been cruel
I never thought of the sculpin
hanging from the line, its pain
or its terror at the white throat
of a brown trout about to swallow, I was a boy
without philosophy, living

in harmony more with nature than humankind
People have returned to fishing, disgusted
with themselves, with others
I'm thinking of trying fishing too
Maybe I'll regain my innocence and breathe again
like the earth in May, maybe
I'll be cured of philanthropy and other big words
from the desire for anarchic revolution
*to drown out the ancient instinct of blood**
As long as I remember
I wanted only one thing
to finally return where I belong
as living being or an electron
to omniscient and terrifying nature.

*   From Stefan Zweig, *The World of Yesterday* (1942)

The Last Judgement of the Ant

The factories and the schools
that were once concentration camps
are factories and schools again
The hotels that were rape camps
are once again hotels
Transport trucks that took away the living
and brought back corpses
are once again transport trucks
bringing everyday
groceries, livestock, tiles, timber, cement
Our forests are again our forests, though
full of the missing
Our rivers are still
wild, green and blue, though they hide
the bones of the innocent
The most fragrant grasses in Europe
grow in our meadows
they grow over mass graves

Abundance is everywhere, nature and society
move on, what used to be sniper alley
is now a perfume store
and again, the devil claims his own
when autumn is long, icy and wet
when endless winter brings fog, snow
nights are darker than despair

and the room is airless
when marathon thoughts outlast every cigarette
the devil taps a branch on the window, the storm
tears leaves, yellow, red and green
sticking them to your face
The devil is true to his word, reminding you
you are still an animal
crawling like a worm, running like a field mouse
dying without glory, your instinct
useless, war is biology, the food chain
the strong eat the weak
If they eat you, you are history
that is the whole truth

Only the soul poses a problem
science can't explain away
She hurts yet you cannot touch her
I don't think a soul can die, it doesn't
fit with cosmic justice
Each time I think I have lost my soul
I can go to Omarska or Potočari
sit amongst the gravestones, stare
at a blade of grass on the mound of an unknown man
at an ant that climbs the smooth headstone
defying gravity, here
I can be purified without torture or fire
I don't burn in the limbo of everyday
I comprehend heaven and earth, fire and water
and know it all must be
renewed, the soul will never die
the body's just its launch pad
That ant on the white granite is Lord of the Universe

a positive force, he decides everything
Him you cannot crush
he will decide your fate at the Last
Judgement, in all courts of law
If factories return to what they used to be
if careless lovers moan in hotel rooms
as trucks distribute human garbage and dust
it does not matter
That ant will decide, he knows it all
he is incorruptible, in this I believe
as sure as I believe in the soul of the world.

Song of the Survivors

Sometimes life has perfect meaning
wherever you look brings back
the harmony which was shaken as we fell
from heaven, a waiter places the sun
umbrella by the ice-cream larder
a turquoise scarf flaps over the river
the day unfolds like Captain Cook's treasure map
excitement up until the sun sets
We search for the purpose of our lives
and then like moles with dim eyes
we crawl into the humus of darkness, the roots
of the cosmos, dark matter
our uterus, all the answers are
found, floating in the foetal position
Each evening a predator arrives
its wings fluttering like silk across a woman's hips
it digs up the loam where we crawled, looking
for answers
As it eats us, our children and our dreams
it says: *look for no answers but me*
When we awake
swollen-eyed from the force of all we've seen
scorched from jumping
through the fiery hoops of cities, we know
history repeats itself, a routine
experiment across our backs

alchemy reversed, traces of cold weaponry
and agricultural tools
mark our indestructible bones
Calcium to calcium
flesh to grass, to mushrooms, wild beasts
Every day ends this way
and begins with perfection
with ice-cream on a stick
with the cheerful bark of a poodle
with the wind in my hair
and genocide forgotten.

The Author

Faruk Šehić was born in 1970 in Bihać. Until the outbreak of war in 1992, Šehić studied Veterinary Medicine in Zagreb. However, the then 22-year-old voluntarily joined the Army of Bosnia and Herzegovina, in which he led a unit of 130 men as a lieutenant. After the war he studied literature and since 1998 has worked as a columnist, author and poet. The literary critics regard him as the voice of the so-called 'mangled generation'. His debut novel *Knjiga o Uni* (2011; *Quiet Flows the Una*, 2016) was awarded the Meša Selimović prize for the best novel published in Serbia, Bosnia and Herzegovina, Montenegro and Croatia in 2011, and EU Prize for Literature 2013. Other notable works of prose include *Pod Pritiskom* (2004; *Under Pressure*, 2019), *Priče sa satnim mehanizmom*, 2018 and *Greta*, 2021.

For his collection of poems in the Italian and Bosnian languages *Ritorno alla natura / Povratak prirodi* he received XXXI Premio Letterario Camaiore – Francesco Belluomini 2019 (Premio Internazionale). His books have been translated into English, Turkish, Slovenian, Hungarian, Italian, Polish, German, Bulgarian, French, Spanish, Dutch, Arab, Romanian and Macedonian. He works in the respected political magazine *BH Dani* as a columnist and journalist.

Faruk Šehić lives in Sarajevo.

The Translator

S.D. Curtis is a sometime author and Chief Editor of Istros Books – a publishing company which she founded to bring the writing and culture of SE Europe to an English-speaking audience. Since it was founded in 2011, Istros' titles have been nominated and shortlisted for the Oxford Weidenfeld Translation Prize, the Warwick Prize for Women's Literature in Translation, the Republic of Consciousness prize, the EBRD Literature prize and the EU Prize for Literature. Curtis studied literature and public art at Roehampton University, holds an MA in Education (Applied Linguistics) has published poetry (*Diary of a Divorce*, Arc Publications, 2020, *The Harvest Journal*, Jung Club London, 2021) as well as translations from Bosnian/Croatian (*New Directions, Istros, Guernica Magazine*).